MILNER CRAFT SERIES

WILDFLOWERS IN CANDLEWICKING

JAN POTTER

SALLY MILNER PUBLISHING

First published in 1995 by
Sally Milner Publishing Pty Ltd
9/44-48 Bowral Street
Bowral NSW 2576 Australia

Reprinted 1996
Reprinted 1999
© Jan Potter, 1995

Cover and design by Anna Warren
Photography by John Hollingshead
Back cover photo by Heather Potter
Photographs styled by Lisa Hilton
Computer drawn illustrations by Anna Warren
Colour separation in Australia by Sphere Color Graphics
Printed in Hong Kong

National Library of Australia
Cataloguing-in-Publication data:

Potter, Jan (Jan Heather).
    Wildflowers in Candlewicking.

    ISBN 1 86351 174 1.

    1. Candlewicking (Embroidery) - Patterns. 2. Decoration and
    ornament - Plant forms. I. Title. (Series : Milner craft series).

746.44

DEDICATION

To my mum, Heather Sheens, a wonderful craftswoman who, through necessity, discovered and grew to love the satisfaction of creating beautiful things. Thank you for sharing this gift with me.

CONTENTS

ACKNOWLEDGEMENTS

Writing a book is like having a baby. In my case the 'baby' went long over term!

During my 'term', I received the assistance of various compassionate and sympathetic people:

• regular visits to 'doctor' Sally Milner provided the encouragement I needed to renew my efforts;

• 'midwife' Shirley of Morisset Fabrics and Crafts, Morisset, NSW, provided a listening ear and wise suggestions;

• Ray, my 'intern', applied regular kickstarts to my flagging labour;

• 'matron' Gay and 'deputy' Ilse sewed the vest;

• my sisters Nerida and Glenda, daughters Lynda, Heather and Karen, friends Jean, Pauline, Bev, Rosalind, Stella, and Ann, my typist, 'nursed' me throughout this arduous passage.

Thank you all – you have shared the agony, now share the ecstasy of the birth of this book...

The following products are shown in the photographs:

White cushions, spectacles and tea cup from Mosman Antique Centre; chair, cushions and throwover from Linen & Lace of Balmain; tablecloth and plates from Mikasa Enterprises; and quilting, scissors and embroidery threads from Lincraft Fabrics.

INTRODUCTION

This book takes a new, colourful look at the beautiful, long-established art of candlewicking.

I have matched new-style threads with beautiful designs of some of the Australian native wildflowers I grew up with, and the results are a departure from traditional cream-on-cream candlewicking.

Candlewicking was born in the Wild West, when women travelling west in wagon trains to discover and open up America's prairies longed for some comfort and adornment in the harsh, lonely places where they found themselves.

Having few of the comforts of home, and rarely able to visit shops, these women developed a way of creating useful and decorative articles for the home using the canvas-like, cream cotton fabric used for the roofs of the wagons and the wicks of candles as threads — also made of cotton and much the same colour.

I like to think of them making rough quilts and table-cloths while thinking about family and friends back home. The longing and homesickness they felt were stitched into simple, beautiful designs and turned into treasured items during quiet, reflective times.

I hope that you will enjoy making these simple candlewicking designs, whether you're surrounded by family members and chatting, or using the time to let your mind wander and roam.

Each project should take no longer than a couple of days, even for a beginner. It takes approximately four to five hours to stitch one of these designs. As the stitches are easy to master, these projects can easily be done while sitting with your family, watching television or listening to music.

Why not make a quilt, incorporating all the designs in this book? By making one design per week — or even two as you get more adept — and some easy blank blocks to go in between, in just four months or so you'll have an elegant and unique quilt.

The designs, fabrics and project ideas in this book are all suggestions and are all interchangeable. So, using this book as a guide, choose your favourite designs and create your own project.

This book is set out so that all the wildflower designs are shown first. Following them are a few ideas for projects you can make using the various designs. Before you start, have a thorough look through the designs, choose one and then choose the item you want to make. Read the instructions for both carefully. Then you will know which materials are required, the techniques involved, the sequence for stitching and where to place your design when transferring it onto the fabric with dressmakers' carbon paper. Make sure your stitches cover all the carbon marks.

Chapter 1
MATERIALS AND EQUIPMENT

FABRICS

Homespun has been used for most of the designs. It's a great fabric to work with, is available in various colours and makes for casual country-style looks at affordable prices.

Linen is also great to work with, but make sure the needle doesn't come up through the same hole. Candlewicking on linen looks very elegant and if you have some old linen, you can make a new/old heirloom.

Voile is a lovely light fabric. Use the lighter, more spaced out designs rather than the closely-stitched ones for best results on this fabric.

Handkerchief lawn looks beautiful with white-on-white embroidery. The honey flower design I chose for the handkerchief is one of my favourite designs. As children we used to pick them and suck out the nectar from the ends.

Velvet is the material I used for the vest (page 13, McCalls 5064 View F). The gum blossoms design looks so rich and lustrous on this fabric that it's hard to go past it, but you could also use khaki-coloured linen or raw silk.

THREADS

This new-look candlewicking uses luscious, lustrous threads in a variety of colours.

I have used mostly Ristal threads, normally used for Brazilian embroidery and smocking. Made from rayon, they are colourfast and easy to work with. These glossy threads really make the wildflowers come to life.

I have also used various brands of stranded cotton: DMC, Coats-Anchor, Madeira, Myart, Semco and Rajmahal Silk.

And some knitting yarns: Sullivans 4-ply Natural Soft Crochet and Knitting cotton, and a 4-ply golden knitting rayon.

NEEDLES

A large-eyed crewel needle is suitable for these projects.

EMBROIDERY HOOPS

You'll need a small 10 cm (4") or 13 cm (5") hoop. A free-standing frame is ideal as it leaves both hands free to manipulate the needle.

A note about the vest (pattern, page 13): no hoop or frame was used on the velvet for fear it would mark, but as part of the collar is cut on the cross, it may stretch or pull without a frame. To counteract this, it may be useful to iron on the interfacing side before embroidering the collar.

TRANSFERRING DESIGNS TO FABRIC

The easiest way of transferring a design onto fabric is to use dressmakers' carbon paper or folk art transfer paper, both of which will wash off easily.

You may find it hard to keep a design on velvet fabric. One way to overcome this is to prick an outline of the design (photocopy it first) with a pin, then lay the pattern down on the fabric and run talcum powder over the holes, leaving dots on the fabric in the shape of the design.

CARE OF THE PIECES

Wash according to washing instructions for the fabric you are using or the thread which you have used.

IRONING

Always iron on the reverse of the embroidered side, resting the fabric on a thick pad of towels.

STITCH TECHNIQUES

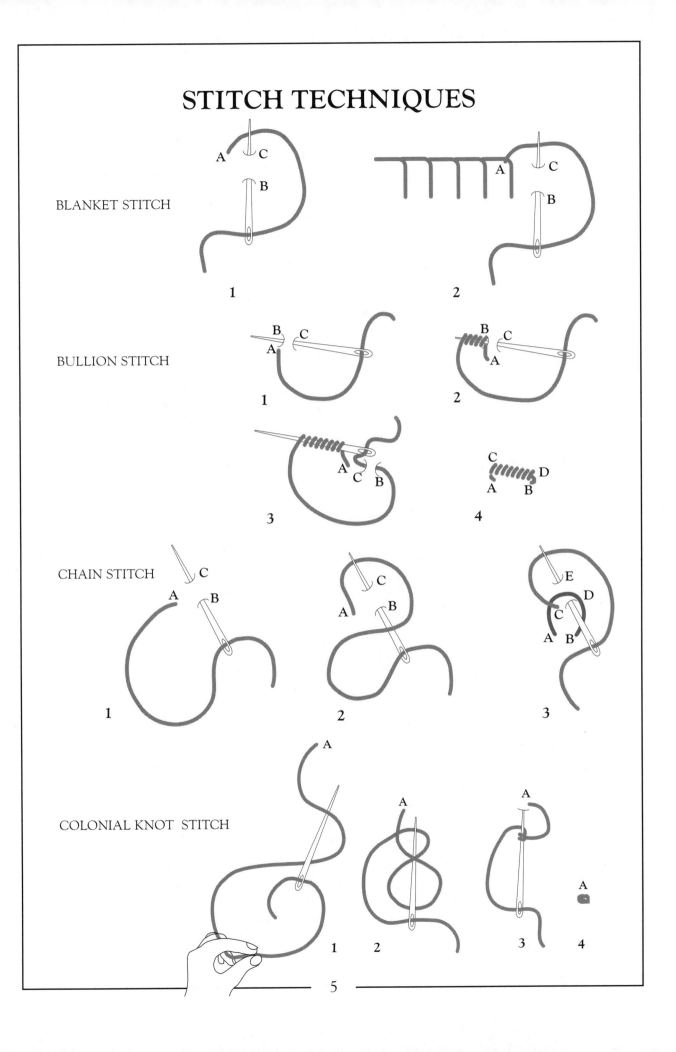

BLANKET STITCH

BULLION STITCH

CHAIN STITCH

COLONIAL KNOT STITCH

CORAL STITCH

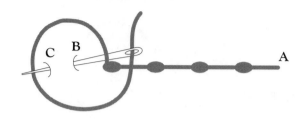

LAZY DAISY

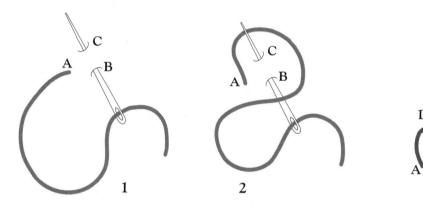

PISTIL STITCH

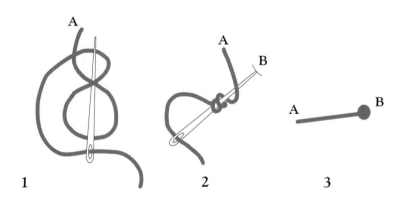

STEM STITCH

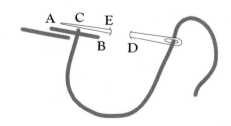

Chapter 2
THE DESIGNS

Note: These designs may be used on any of the projects, or may be adapted to anything the reader wishes to try.

Bottlebrush

This design is used for a small cushion and a tea cosy.

REQUIREMENTS
Ristal threads: Lola 065, 110, 210; Iris 044, 163, 205

METHOD

Trace the design onto chosen fabric with dressmakers' carbon paper.

Colonial knots, pistil stitch, lazy daisy stitch and stem stitch are used in this design.

- **Stems**: Using Lola 210, stitch a single row of colonial knots along the design lines.
- **Centre rib of flowers:** Using Lola 210, stem stitch the very centre rib of the flowers. Using Iris 044, stitch a single row of colonial knots on each side of the stem stitching to form the buds for the stamens.
- **Leaves:** Using Lola 110 and lazy daisy stitch, embroider leaves on stems and at tips of flowers.
- **Bottlebrushes:**
  Flower 1: Using Iris 205 and pistil stitch, embroider only a few random stitches (these are the stamens).
  Flower 2: Using Iris 205 and pistil stitch, embroider every second knot with stitches of varying lengths.
  Flowers 3 and 4: Using Iris 163 and pistil stitch, embroider on every second knot along the centre with stitches of varying lengths.
  Flower 5: Using Lola 065, embroider every second knot along the centre with stitches of varying lengths.

Christmas Bells

This design is used for a small piece for framing.

REQUIREMENTS
Ristal threads: Frost 069, 080; Lola 065

METHOD
Trace the design onto chosen fabric with dressmakers' carbon paper.

   Colonial knots are used in this design.

- **Flower and bud tips:** Using Frost 069 and colonial knots, fill in the points of the flower and tips of the buds. Scatter some knots into the body of the flower, above the filled-in points, to show that the yellow runs into the red of the flower.

Jan Potter
© 1993

- **Main body of flowers and buds:** Using Lola 065 and colonial knots, fill in the main part of the buds and flowers. If you want the flowers to appear as though they are reflecting the light, embroider a patch on each flower using the lighter threads, remembering that the light will come from one direction only.
- **Leaves and stems:** Using Frost 080 and colonial knots, embroider the tops of the stems with a single line of knots and stitch a double row of knots for the lower parts of the stems.

Teapot cosy and tray cloth
Inset: Detail of honey flower on tray cloth

Framed Christmas bells

Top: Trio of drumsticks being worked. A single
design used 3 times
Bottom: Bottlebrush cushion, flannel flower cushion,
gum blossom cushion

Tablecloth with flannel flowers and tassels

Drumstick

This design is used for a linen tray cloth and a patchwork block.

REQUIREMENTS
Ristal threads: Frost 008, 069, 080; Iris 044

METHOD
Trace the design onto chosen fabric with dressmakers' carbon paper.

Colonial knots and pistil stitch are used in this design.

- **Stem:** Using Iris 044, embroider a double row of colonial knots along the design lines.
- **Leaves:** Using Frost 080, stitch a single row of colonial knots along the design lines.
- **Flower centre:** Using Frost 069 or 080, or both, fill in the centre with colonial knots.
- **Outer parts of the flower:** These look like stamens. Embroider them in layers of pistil stitch, following the design outlines.

Flannel Flowers

This design is used for a table cloth and an appliqué square for a small cushion.

REQUIREMENTS
Ristal threads: Lola 010, 110, 165

METHOD
Trace the design onto chosen fabric with dressmakers' carbon paper.

Satin stitch, colonial knots, bullion stitch and coral stitch are used in this design.

- **Flower petals:** Using Lola 010 and satin stitch, fill in each petal. Using Lola 110, bullion stitch the outer end of each petal.
- **Flower centres:** Using Lola 165, pack the centres with colonial knots so there are no gaps. Using Lola 225, scatter 3 or 5 knots in each of the centres.
- **Stems:** Using Lola 110, coral stitch along the stem lines.
- **Leaves:** Using Lola 110, stitch colonial knots along the outline of the leaves. Using Lola 165, embroider colonial knots in masses inside and outside these outlines.

Gum Blossoms

This design is used for a small cushion and a velvet waist-coat (McCalls pattern 5064 view F). This design can be used on one cushion four times to form a circle, or in the corner of a cushion.

REQUIREMENTS
Ristal threads: Lola 030, 065, 110; Iris 044, 205

METHOD

Trace the design onto chosen fabric with dressmakers' carbon paper. Sage green homespun fabric is recommended for the cushion, black velvet for the vest.

Colonial knots, blanket stitch, stem stitch, pistil stitch and satin stitch are used in this design.

- **Large leaves:** Using Lola 110, blanket stitch along one outer edge of the leaves. The 'legs' of the blanket stitch will form the veins of the leaf. Stitch colonial knots along the central vein and the other edge of the leaf.
- **Small leaves:** Using Lola 110, stem stitch along the central vein and one outer edge of the leaf. Embroider the other edge with colonial knots.
- **Stem and twigs:** Using Iris 044, stitch a single row of colonial knots for all stems and twigs, following the design outlines.
- **Nuts:** Using Lola 065 at the stem end of the nuts, embroider 2 colonial knots. Then, using Lola 030 at the top half of the nuts, embroider 1 or 3 colonial knots, depending on size.
- **Flower cups:** Using Iris 044, embroider satin stitch across the cup from side to side.
- **Flowers:** Using Iris 205, start each flower with a full layer of pistil stitch. Then, using Lola 065, embroider another full layer of pistil stitch over the top.
- **Scrolls:** Using Lola 110, stitch a single row of colonial knots along the design lines. (As seen in the colour photograph.)

Honey Flower

(Mountain Devil)

This design is used for a handkerchief, cushion and linen tray cloth.

REQUIREMENTS
Ristal threads: Lola 120; Frost 069, 080, 205
On the handkerchief only white 000 was used

METHOD
Trace the design onto chosen fabric with dressmakers' carbon paper.
   Colonial knots, pistil stitch and stem stitch are used in this design.

- **Stem:** Using Lola 120, stitch a single row of colonial knots along the design outlines.
- **Leaves:** Using Frost 080, coral stitch along the design outlines only.
- **Outer flower petals:** Using Frost 205, stem stitch the lower half of all petals. Using Frost 069, stem stitch the upper half of all petals.
- **Stamens:** Using Frost 205 double thread, pistil stitch all the stamens between the petals. To avoid long threads at the back of the fabric, bring the needle to the front, near the top of the pistil stitch. Make a long stitch to help fill in the gaps. Take the needle through to the back to finish off the long stitch, then come to the front again, next to the end of the long stitch, to start a new pistil stitch. Using the double thread, make extra colonial knots at the knot end of the pistil stitch. Make an uneven one or two rows, depending on how long the pistil stitch was made.

  Using a single thread of Frost 205, embroider 3 or 4 small stamens in pistil stitch protruding from the top of the main stamens.

  Alternatively, use knitting cotton in the same colours, as shown in the colour photograph.
- **Leaves:** Pistil or coral stitch end to end.
- **Outer petals:** Fill in with continuous chain stitch or stem stitch.
- **Stamens:** As per above instructions.
- **Frame:** Lightly rule a parallel line approximately 6 cm ($2\frac{3}{8}$") in from the bottom and the top of the cushion. Approximately 8 cm ($3\frac{1}{8}$") in from the sides of the cushion lightly pencil two lines which meet the other two lines. Embroider two rows of pistil stitch end to end around the frame. First embroider a single row, then turn and come back for a second row.

Lilly Pilly

This design is used for a large cushion.

REQUIREMENTS
Ristal threads: Iris 044, Frost 000, 043, 069
Rajamahal Silk 200 can be used in place of Frost 043

METHOD
Trace the design onto the centre of chosen fabric using dressmakers' carbon paper. White homespun fabric is recommended.

Colonial knots, pistil stitch and coral stitch are used in this design.

- **Leaves:** Using Iris 044, outline the leaves with a single line of colonial knots, including the stems and the central veins.
- **Flowers:** Using Frost 043 (or Rajamahal Silk 200), lay a base of pistil stitch stamens. Then top with another layer of pistil stitch using Frost 000. Using Frost 069, stitch the centres of the flowers and the actual flower cups with colonial knots.
- **Frame:** Fold the embroidered fabric square in half horizontally, then vertically. Mark the mid-points of each side with a pin. Measure in 2 cm (¾") from the pins and mark with a light dot using a pencil. With a ruler and pencil, lightly draw two parallel lines 1 cm (⅜") apart connecting the four dots, forming a diamond-shaped frame around the flowers. Embroider the frame using Frost 000 with coral stitch. Make sure the thread is pulled with even tension between the knots, otherwise it will look loopy.

Many-flowered Fringed Violet

This design is used for a small cushion and voile table throwover. See page 27 for the design used for the throwover.

REQUIREMENTS
Ristal threads: Lola 041, 110, 059, 127; Frost 044 (if unavailable, use 050 or 080)
Alternatively, you can use: Madeira (Greens) 1408, 1410, 1411; Anchor (Greens) 0279, 1280; (Purples) 086, 096; Semco (Purples) 998; (Browns) 963; DMC (Yellows) 3078; (Browns) 976

METHOD

Trace the design onto chosen fabric with dressmaker's carbon paper.

Colonial knots, bullion stitch, blanket stitch and coral stitch are used in this design.

- **Stems:** Using Lola 110, stitch single rows of colonial knots along the design outlines.
- **Buds:** Using Lola 110, make the buds in bullion stitch. Depending on the size of the bud, do 6-10 wraps per bud using a single straight stitch to join the buds to the stems.
- **Grass:** Using Frost 044 (alternatively you can use Frost 050 or 080 or a mixture of them), do single rows of colonial knots along each stem of grass.
- **Flowers:** Using Lola 127, do the petals in bullion stitch with between 6 and 12 wraps, depending on the size of the petals. Using Lola 041, do a blanket stitch around the outside of each bullion stitch. The 'head' of the blanket stitch should surround the bullion stitch, while the 'legs' of the blanket stitch should form at the edge of the petal.
- **Background tree:** Using Lola 059, outline the tree with a single row of colonial knots.
- **Foreground rocks and twigs:** Using Lola 059, outline the rocks and twigs with a single row of colonial knots and/or coral stitch.
- **Circular frame:** Using Lola 110, do a single row of coral stitch.

Trigger Flowers

This design is used for a small cushion.

REQUIREMENTS
Ristal threads: Lola 000, 010, 043, 050, 059, 083.
Alternatively, you can use Myart rayon: 183, 189, 190, 199; Madeira 1410, 1411; DMC 69

METHOD

Trace the design onto the centre of chosen fabric with dressmaker's carbon paper. White homespun fabric is recommended.

Colonial knots, pistil stitch, stem stitch, coral stitch and bullion stitch are used in this design.

- **Leaves:** Using Lola 050, stem stitch the two middle leaves. Using Lola 050, coral stitch all the other leaves.
- **Stems:** Using Lola 059, stem stitch each stem in full.
- **Flowers:** Using Lola 043 and 083, embroider colonial knots in groups of 2 and 4 for the individual flowers with long stems. Then using Lola 010 and pistil stitch, embroider trigger stamens from each group of knots. Using Lola 043 and 083, embroider 9 bullion stitches with 6 wraps each to form a cone shape at the top of the flowers.
- **Frame:** Fold the embroidered fabric square in half horizontally, then vertically. Mark the mid-points of each side with a pin. Measure in 2 cm (¾") from the pins and mark with a light dot using a pencil. With a ruler and pencil, lightly rule straight lines connecting the four dots, forming a diamond-shaped frame around the flowers. Embroider the frame, using Lola 000 with coral stitch. Make sure the thread is pulled with even tension between the knots, otherwise it will look loopy.

Waratah

This design is used for an appliqué square on a small cushion.

REQUIREMENTS
Ristal threads: Lola 065, 110; Iris 044

METHOD
Trace the design onto chosen fabric using dressmakers' carbon paper. Dark green homespun is recommended.

Colonial knots and blanket stitch are used in this design.

- **Stem:** Using Iris 044, stitch two rows of colonial knots following the design outlines.
- **Leaves:** Using Lola 110, stitch colonial knots following the design outlines. Blanket stitch to the left and right of central veins for additional veins.
- **Flower:** Using Lola 065, embroider the flower in a mass of knots. If you want the flower to appear as if it is reflecting the light, embroider a patch on it using the light threads, as shown in the colour photograph.
- **Leaves at flower base:** Using Lola 110, stitch colonial knots, following the design outlines. Using Lola 065, stitch a second row of colonial knots inside the green row.

Wattle

This design is used for a small cushion, hand-towel edge and tissue box.

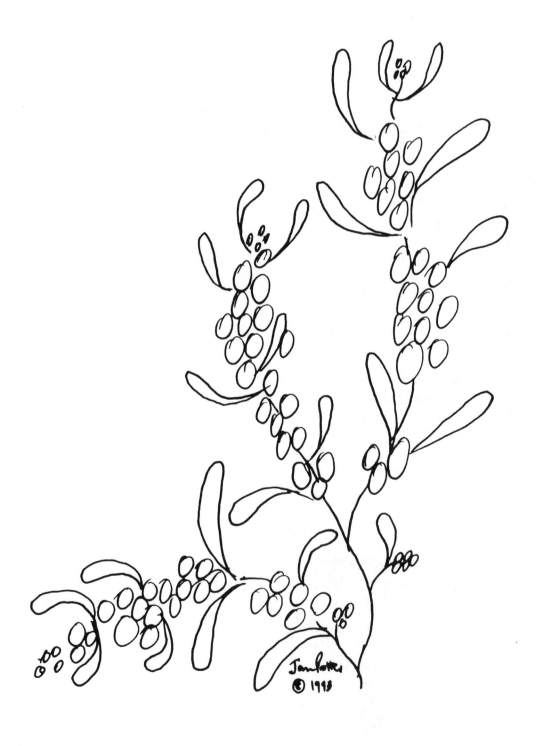

REQUIREMENTS
Ristal thread: Lola 110 green
1 ball rayon knitting yarn in a deep gold colour or 1 ball
(50 g) Sullivans Natural Soft Crochet and Knitting cotton,
4-ply, natural 40201
The alternative yellows, Lola 008, 073, 113, 203, can be
used in place of gold rayon knitting yarn.

METHOD
Trace the design onto centre of chosen fabric with dressmaker's carbon paper.

Colonial knots, coral stitch, satin stitch and chain
stitch are used in this design.

- **Stems:** Using Lola 110, stitch a single row of colonial knots along the design lines.
- **Leaves:** Using Lola 110, outline each leaf using
  coral stitch.
- **Flowers:** Using rayon knitting yarn, loosely fill in
  the blossom areas with colonial knots. For the larger blossoms near beginning of stems, use four
  threads; for medium blossoms, use two threads.
  For small blossoms at the very end of the stems,
  use one thread. Alternatively, stitch the whole
  design using the natural knitting cotton.
- **Frame:** Measure 4 cm (1½") in from each side of
  fabric square and lightly pencil in a square.
  Measure 4 cm (1½") along each line from the four
  corners and mark with a light dot. Join the dots on
  adjoining lines with a diagonal line, cutting the corners as in the diagram below. Coral stitch along
  lines to form a hexagon around the design, using
  the gold rayon knitting yarn. This frame is to be
  added to the design if making a cushion.

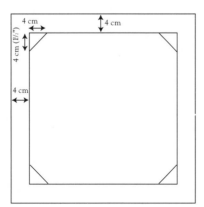

Chapter 3
THE PROJECTS

Table Throwover

Suitable design: many-flowered fringed violet.

REQUIREMENTS
1 m (40") square of voile
4 m (4 ½ yd) fine white cotton lace

METHOD
Turn in the edges of the voile square and sew with a straight stitch.

Using a fine zigzag setting, stitch the lace to the edges, easing around the corners.

Velvet waistcoat with gum blossom

Tissue box cover, appliqué hand towel with wattle,
handkerchief with crocheted edge and honey flowers

Top: Large cushion with lilly pilly, small cushion
with trigger flowers
Bottom: Voile throwover with many flowered
fringed violets

Wattle cushion with cream and coloured embroidery,
cushion appliquéd with waratah embroidery

Design used for table throwover

Appliqué Hand Towel

Suitable design: wattle.

REQUIREMENTS
45 cm x 13 cm (17¾" x 5⅛") strip of homespun fabric (for embroidery)
1 m (40") tartan piping
1 hand towel

METHOD
Sew tartan piping on the wrong sides of long edges of homespun fabric.

Lay fabric face down on the wrong side of the hand towel, parallel to and 5 cm (2") above bottom edge of towel.

Sew short ends of fabric to edges of towel.

Turn right side out.

Sew fabric to towel on right side, close to the piping.

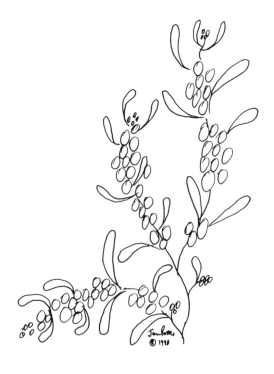

Large Tassels

Approximately 7.5 cm (3") long.

REQUIREMENTS
4-ply knitting cotton, natural colour
Heavy cardboard strip, approximately 7.5 cm (3") wide

METHOD
Wind knitting cotton around the cardboard strip 100 times.

Tie tightly at one edge with a length of cotton, leaving these ends long. These will be used later to attach the tassel.

Cut at the other edge.

Bind tightly 1.5 cm (⅝") from the top of tied end, using another length of cotton.

Trim to make bottom ends even.

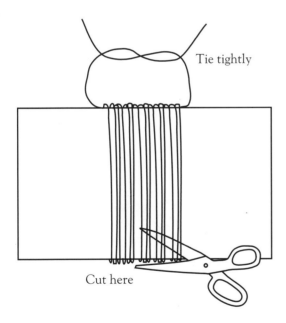

Tie tightly

Cut here

Wind and tie tightly

Trim ends

Table Cloth

Suitable design: flannel flowers.

REQUIREMENTS
110 cm x 110 cm (43¼" x 43¼") cream homespun fabric
2 cm x 4.5 m (¾" x 5 yd) cream satin bias binding
4.5 m (5 yd) pale green cord

METHOD
Sew the bias around the outside edge of homespun fabric, putting the wrong sides together.

Press up to the right side and mitre the corners by hand. (Instructions on how to mitre corners can be found on page 40.)

As shown in the diagram, lay the cord along the edge of the bias and, beginning at one corner, zigzag over the cord, catching the edge of the bias as you go.

Sew one large tassel on each corner.

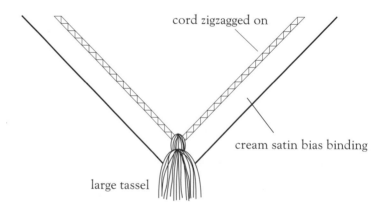

cord zigzagged on

cream satin bias binding

large tassel

Cushion

Suitable designs: many-flowered fringed violet, wattle, bottlebrush, trigger flowers, flannel flowers, lilly pilly, waratah, gum blossoms and honey flower.

REQUIREMENTS
For a large cushion:
Two pieces of 36 cm x 36 cm (14¼" x 14¼") fabric
35 cm (14") pillow form
32 cm (12½") zip

For a small cushion:
Two pieces of 32 cm x 32 cm (12½" x 12½") fabric
30 cm (12") pillow form
25 cm (10") zip

METHOD
Place the right sides of the fabric together.
Sew three seams in overlock or straight stitch and zigzag.
    Turn to right side and insert the zip with teeth showing.

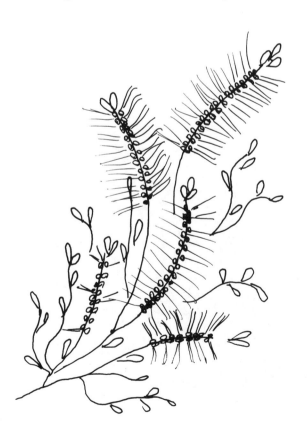

Appliqué Cushion

Suitable designs: flannel flowers and waratah.

REQUIREMENTS
Two pieces of 32 cm x 32 cm (12 ½" x 12 ½") fabric.
One piece of 16 cm x 18 cm (6 ¼" x 7") contrasting homespun fabric (for embroidery)
2 cm x 72 cm (¾" x 28 ⅜") cream bias binding

METHOD
Centre and zigzag the embroidered patch onto the front of
the larger piece of fabric.
　Beginning at the centre bottom of patch and turning
cut edge of bias back, sew inside-out around the edge of
patch.
　Turn bias over onto front of patch and sew down on
the right side to make a frame for the patch.
　If using the waratah design, sew wooden buttons onto
the corners of the frame.

Small Tassels

Approximately 4 cm (1½") long.

REQUIREMENTS
To make 2 tassels:
Ecru pearl cotton
Heavy cardboard strip, approximately 8 cm (3⅛") wide

METHOD
Wind ecru pearl cotton around the cardboard strip 100 times.

Tie tightly at each edge with a length of cotton, leaving these ends long. These will be used later to attach the tassel.

Cut threads at the centre of the cardboard strip.

Bind tightly about 1 cm (⅜") down from tied end, using another length of cotton.

Trim to make bottom ends even.

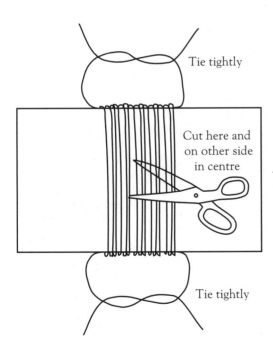

Tie tightly

Cut here and on other side in centre

Tie tightly

Wind and tie tightly

Trim ends

Crochet Edge for Handkerchief

Suitable design: honey flower.

REQUIREMENTS
No 1.00 steel hook
No 80 DMC crochet thread
20 cm x 20 cm (8" x 8") hem-stitched handkerchief
Simple block pattern, in multiples of 3

METHOD
Crochet around the edge of the handkerchief in the following pattern:

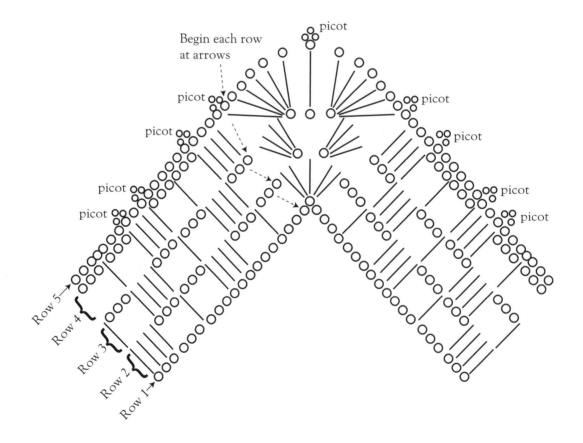

Row 1 Double crochet around handkerchief in multiples of 3.

Row 2   (3ch, 1tr, 3ch, 4tr) repeat to corner, 3ch. Into corner chain make 2tr, 1ch, 1tr, 1ch, 2tr. Continue other side as before, repeating ( ).

Row 3   (3ch, 4tr, 3ch, 1tr) repeat to corner. 3ch, miss 2tr, make 4 tr in next chain. Continue side as before, repeating ( ).

Row 4   (4tr, 3ch, 1tr, 3ch) repeat to corner. 4tr in each of the next chains. Miss next 4 tr in previous row, crochet 6tr in next chain, 1tr in second chain, 6tr in third chain. Continue side as before, repeating ( ).

Row 5   To make a picot edge: double crochet around edge, making a 3ch picot at each end of the treble blocks and at the beginning, middle and end of the corner fan shape, as shown in the diagram on page 34.

Tissue Box Cover

Suitable design: wattle. Pattern will fit a box of 200 tissues.

REQUIREMENTS
Two pieces of 32 cm x 17 cm (12½" x 6¾") of homespun fabric (for embroidery)
Two pieces of 9 cm x 26 cm (3½" x 10¼") fabric for top of underskirt
One piece of 85 cm x 18 cm (33½" x 7") fabric for sides of underskirt
2 m (2¼ yd) tartan piping
75 cm (29½") knicker elastic

METHOD

1 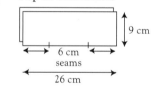 Embroidered pieces with tartan piping

2a Top of underskirt

2b Wrong side of top of underskirt opened out

3 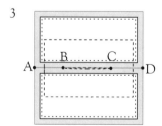 X-ray view of embroidered pieces on top of underskirt. Wrong sides together. Top sew onto underskirt and around embroidered pieces next to piping. Hand sew embroidered pieces together at back between A and B and C and D. Leave gap between B and C for tissues to come out.

4  Underskirt band (for sides) 85 cm x 18 cm (33½" x 7"). Join 18 cm (7") sides with a seam. Join underskirt top (diagram 3) to underskirt band (diagram 4) to form sides of cover. Turn 1 cm (³⁄₈") casing around bottom and insert elastic.

Teapot Cosy

Suitable design: bottlebrush.

REQUIREMENTS
50 cm (19¾") cream homespun fabric
25 cm x 65 cm (10" x 25½") wadding
1.2 m (4 ft approx) cord

METHOD
1 Fold the homespun in half lengthways, then fold ends towards middle. Place pattern upright and cut through 4 layers of fabric.
2 Fold sides of wadding piece to centre. Lay pattern with centre front on fold to cut.
3 Make a wadding sandwich with the wadding inside the homespun circle and the fold at the base. Overlock, or straight sew with zigzag, the pieces together along the curved edge.
4 With right sides of each wadded piece together, sew around curved edges.
5 Turn right side out and hand sew cord to seam using a hemming stitch.

Make two small 6 cm (2⅜") loops with a 10 cm (4") loop in between at the top as you sew around.

Use about 15 cm (6") of cord to make a knotted tie hanging from the top.

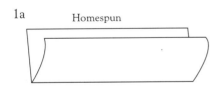

1a   Homespun

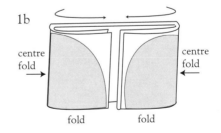

1b

centre fold   centre fold

fold   fold

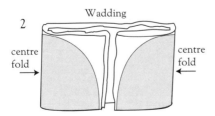

2   Wadding

centre fold   centre fold

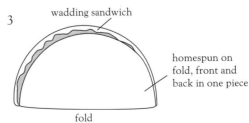

3   wadding sandwich

homespun on fold, front and back in one piece

fold

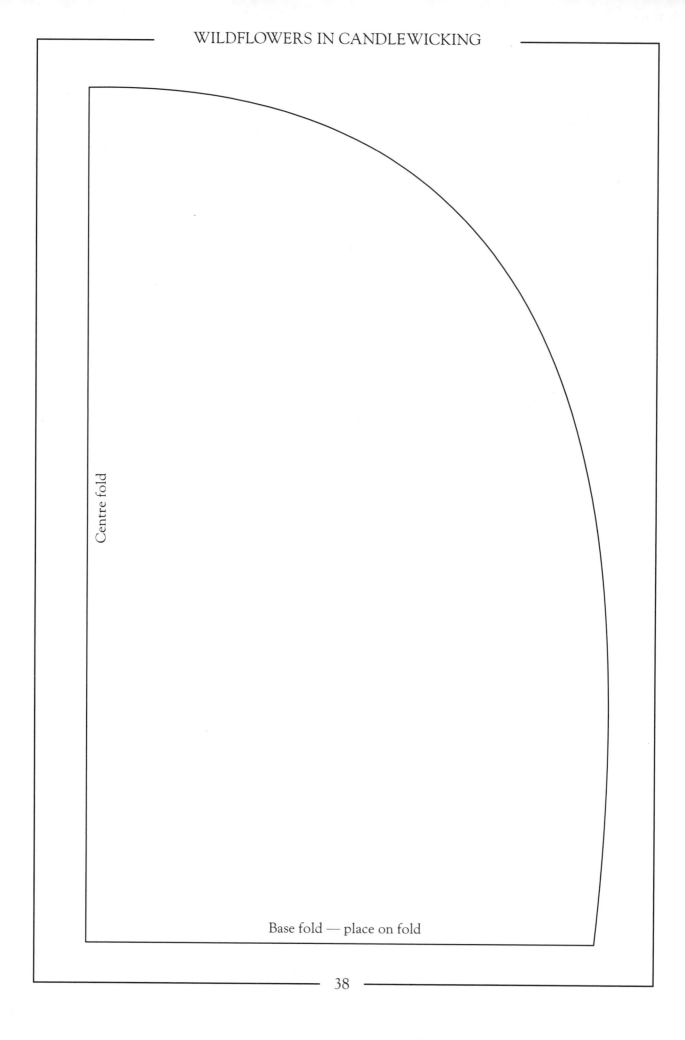

Centre fold

Base fold — place on fold

Quilt Block

Suitable for all the designs found in this book.

REQUIREMENTS
16 cm x 19 cm (6¼" x 7½") homespun fabric patch (for
embroidery)
65 cm (25½") tartan piping
5 cm (2") wide strips of homespun (8 per block)
16 cm x 19 cm (6¼" x 7½") wadding

METHOD
1 Embroider the patch of 16 cm x 19 cm (6¼" x 7½")
  homespun fabric.
2 Begin at one of the lower corners and sew on tartan
  piping, overlapping at final corner.
3 Hand sew wadding with close, small tacking stitches
  hidden under the piping on the right side of the
  patch.
4 Sew a 5 cm (2") strip (right sides together) across the
  top of the patch. Cut off excess. Fold out and iron
  seam.

   Sew a second strip at the end of the first strip,
down the side of the patch. Fold out and iron seam.

   Continue in this fashion till two rows of strips have
been sewn around the patch in log cabin formation.

To use this as a cushion or backed quilt block, cut a
piece of homespun 30 cm x 30 cm and another piece
of wadding 30 cm x 30 cm (12" x 12").

   Sew all three pieces together, that is the quilt block,
wadding and plain backing.

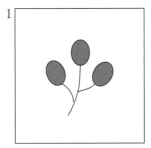

Embroider patch

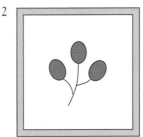

Sew tartan piping to
right side

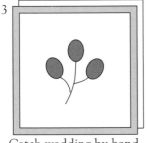

Catch wadding by hand
to back of patch

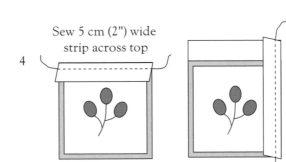

Sew 5 cm (2") wide
strip across top

Sew another
5 cm (2") wide
strip along side

Tray Cloths

Suitable designs: drumstick.

REQUIREMENTS
For a large cloth:
One piece of 50 cm x 40 cm (19¾" x 15¾") linen

For a small cloth:
One piece of 40 cm x 25 cm (15¾" x 10") linen

METHOD
Embroider the design in the appropriate position.

Turn hems to right sides 2 cm (¾") wide, plus a 5 mm (³⁄₁₆") underturn for raw edge.

Pin, tack and mitre corners, and blind hem stitch into place.

TO MITRE CORNERS

1 Fold edge of fabric down 5 mm (³⁄₁₆"), turn under and press.
   Fold a 2 cm (¾") main hem and press.
   Unfold the hem once and draw a diagonal line on the wrong side at point of hemline.
   Cut off the corner leaving 5 mm (³⁄₁₆") seam allowance.
2 Fold back the corner with right sides together and pin and stitch along the marked diagonal line.
3 Turn corner right side out, press and finish hem with blind hem stitching.

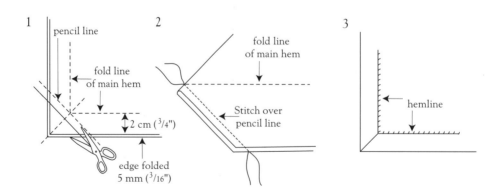